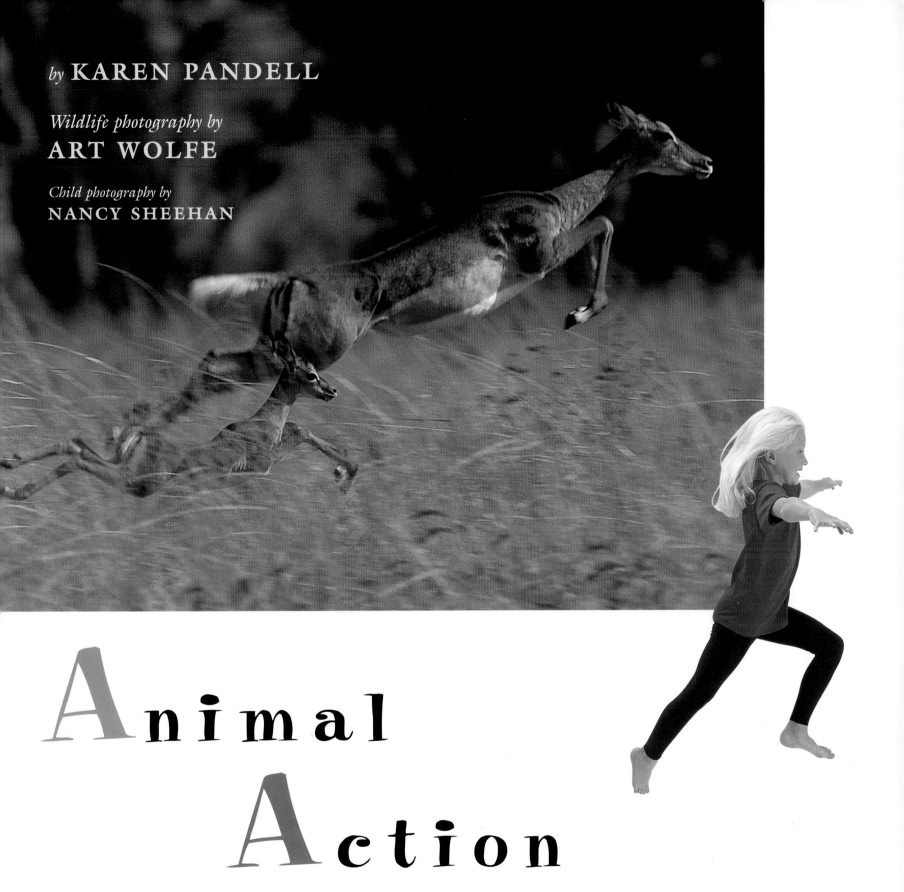

by KAREN PANDELL

Wildlife photography by
ART WOLFE

Child photography by
NANCY SHEEHAN

Animal

Action

ABC

Dutton Children's Books
NEW YORK

DEPICTED ON

jacket front: cheetah *(Acinonyx jubatus)*

title page: impala *(Aepyceros melampus)*

copyright page: red-eyed tree frog *(Agaslychnis callidryas)*

dedication page: slender loris *(Loris tardigradus)*

The photographers and the publisher would like to thank Ray Pfortner, Gavriel Jecan, Chris Eckoff, Melissa Davey, Paula Fillippi, and Kathleen Schiffmann for their invaluable support during the making of this book.

Library of Congress Cataloging-in-Publication Data
Pandell, Karen.   Animal Action ABC / by Karen Pandell; wildlife photography by Art Wolfe;
child photography by Nancy Sheehan. – 1st ed.   p.   cm.
Summary: Rhyming verses beginning with each letter of the alphabet describe movements of a wide range of animals.   ISBN 0–525–45486–1 (hc)
1. Animals—Juvenile literature. 2. Animal mechanics—Juvenile literature. 3. English language—Alphabet—Juvenile literature.
[1. Animals—Miscellanea. 2. Alphabet.] I. Wolfe, Art, ill. II. Sheehan, Nancy, ill.
III. Title QL49.P2535 1996 591—dc20   [E]   96–14191 CIP AC

Published in the United States 1996 by Dutton Children's Books,
a division of Penguin Books USA Inc. • 375 Hudson Street, New York, New York 10014
Art direction by Sara Reynolds • Designed by Semadar Megged
Expert verification by Robert Moore and the resources of the University of Nevada Reno
Printed in Hong Kong   First Edition
10 9 8 7 6 5 4 3 2 1

Children's clothes provided by: After the Stork (800-333-5437)   Biobottoms, Inc. Fresh Air Wear (800-766-1254)   Hanna Andersson (800-222-0544)

We would like to thank the following models: Joseph Basile   Bridget Carroll   Colleen Carroll   Alexandra Dorestant   John Peter Driscoll   Jonathan Fonvielle
Katie Hatfield   Emily Hsu   Purnam Jantrania   Ariana Johnston   Brad Johnston   Taylor Ocko   Whitney Ocko   Anthony Pastore   Jackye Pearson
Alvin Pimentel   Nicholas Rose   Jimmy Silva   Julie Silva   Ricky Silva   Katelyn Tarpey   Aisha Townes   Lenny Turner   Pam Turner   Alice Vu   Van Vu

For Rob
K.P.

To my mother, Eleanor Wolfe
A.W.

To my wonderful sister Mary, who continues to inspire me in my work
N.S.

A r c h

Arch your back and stretch your limbs
Your body forms a tail
Diving deep into the sea
Just like a humpback whale

Balance gracefully

on one leg

Till you become a crane

Then begin

a joyful dance

Flapping your

wings

again and again

*B*alance

Charge

Charge silently

toward your prey

In a sneak attack

But jaguars can be

stalked as well—

Be sure to

watch

your

back!

D r i n k bent over like a giraffe

To give the water a lick

You spread your legs and flex your neck

It's quite an amazing trick!

Drink

E at

E a t just as

a panda does

Grasping with

your paws

The many tasty,

fresh green stalks

You grind

between

your

jaws

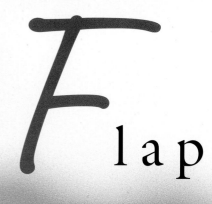

F l a p

F l a p your

outstretched arms

like wings

Beat them like

a macaw

Flying with

your flock

by day

To a cliff

of clay

you saw

G r o w l throughout the forest

Like a grizzly bear

Next you'll sniff, then listen for sounds

To learn who else is there

Growl

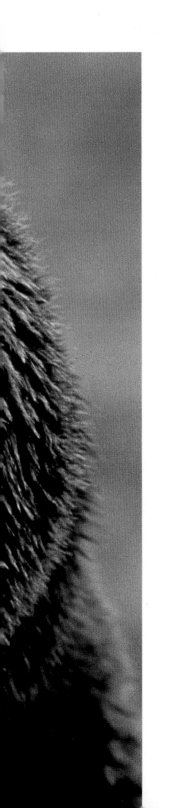

H o w l

H o w l

like a wolf pup

To your sister

or brother

Soon the whole pack

will join in

Singing to one another

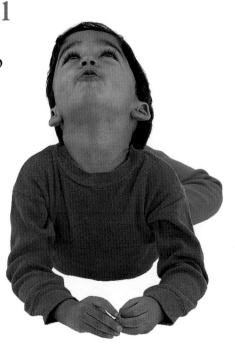

Inflate

Inflate

like a frigatebird

Your throat's a red balloon

Drum your beak

upon this pouch

And make a rhythmic tune

Jump like an impala

Springing high into the air

You bound five, six,

then seven times

Fleeing dangers

everywhere

Jump

Kick like a kangaroo

You want to get

your way

But soon

you'll stop

and save

this fight

Until

another

day

 ick

Leap and **March**

like penguins

Over snow and ice

You are birds that cannot fly

So company is nice!

Leap

March

N a p like a leopard

Resting all the day

After sunset is the time

When you will

hunt and

play

N a p

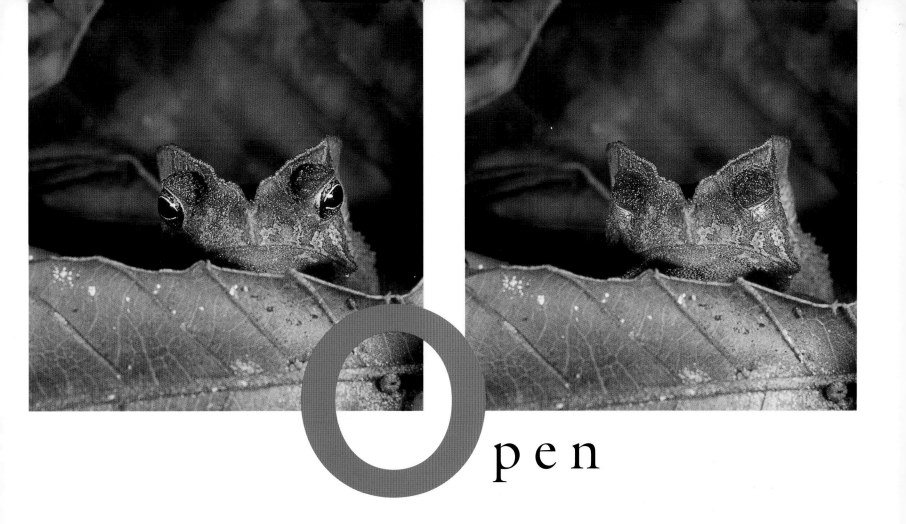

O p e n

O p e n your eyes to scan the forest—

You can hide if you hold still

But close your eyes

and just like magic

You're

invisible!

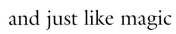

Peek

Peek like an

orangutan

You're often very shy

Was that some sign

of danger

That you saw from

way up high?

Quack

Quack loudly as you waddle

And toddle like a duck

To find a pond in which to swim

You'll walk through sticky muck

R ide

Ride like

a young gorilla

Balanced on

Mama's back

Even when you sleep,

you cling—

You've really

got the knack!

Stretch

out every muscle

And give

a chirping call

When you want

to hunt your prey

You'll sprint

the fastest of all!

tretch

Trumpet

Unfold

Unfold

your wings

and get ready

to fly

While

hanging

by your toes

In the dark,

to find some figs,

Rely upon

your nose

Trumpet

like an elephant

Then shower

with your trunk

You spray your back

to wash it off

With water

you might have

drunk

Vault

like a cougar

Landing soft on

padded feet

You're a

sneaky hunter

No small

creature wants

to meet!

Vault

Wrestle

Wrestle

like two tigers

Grappling with each other

But soon you'll stop

to stare at

And honor

one another

BoX each other, paw to paw

For now, you're matching wits

But arctic hares will really fight

When warmer weather hits!

Yawn

Yawn

Yawn
like a hippo
Open your mouth
up wide
Underwater you stay
all day
This is
where
you
hide

Zap

Zap

an insect with

your tongue

Finally you're

a chameleon

You've acted

your way

from

A to Z

So please

come

celebrate

with me!

NATURE NOTES FOR OLDER READERS

Because many organizations and governments throughout the world keep track of wild animals, population estimates for a species can sometimes differ. For this book, the two sources cited are the Endangered Species List, prepared by the United States Fish and Wildlife Service, and the Red List, designated by the International Union for the Conservation of Nature and Natural Resources (IUCN), a worldwide organization with headquarters in Switzerland.

Bat, epauletted fruit *(Epomophorus wahlbergi)*

 Found mostly in eastern and southeastern Africa

 Fruit bats roost in groups of from three to one hundred individuals. They are especially fond of sweet and juicy figs. They usually visit a number of trees per night to get enough to eat. To find ripe trees, fruit bats primarily use their sense of smell. However, they do rely somewhat on their vision as well. After each nightly meal, fruit seeds pass through the bats' systems undigested. These seeds fall to the ground as the bats fly and help regenerate the forest.

Bear, grizzly; also known as brown bear *(Ursus arctos)* **T**

 Varies from tundra to northern rain forests and coastal areas; found in northwestern North America, Eurasia, and northern Asia

 Grizzlies are powerful animals, strong enough to tear apart steel bolts with their claws. When angry, they can charge an enemy at thirty miles per hour. Since their eyesight is poor, they must rely on their very keen senses of smell and hearing to find food and avoid danger.

Chameleon, Parson's *(Chamaeleo parsonii)*

 Rain forests in Madagascar

 The one commonly known fact about chameleons is that they can change color. Layers of special color cells in a chameleon's skin can shrink or expand to create the appearance of different hues. This creature has other amazing features. Each of its eyes is able to move separately. The tongues of certain species shoot out to farther than the length of their bodies. In this way, slow-moving chameleons can catch food even from a distance.

Cheetah *(Acinonyx jubatus)* **T**

 Africa south of the Sahara, Iran, and possibly parts of Pakistan

 The cheetah is the fastest animal on land. It can sprint to about sixty miles an hour. Its rate of acceleration easily compares with that of a high-powered sports car! Of course, the cheetah can maintain this rate of speed only for short distances. That is why it stalks its prey before attacking. People have long admired this sleek animal. Cheetahs were first tamed for hunting more than four thousand years ago.

Cougar *(Felis concolor)* **E**

 Mountainous, forested, and swampy areas in the western United States and Canada as well as arid bush country, with small, isolated populations in Florida, Tennessee, Alabama, and Louisiana

 Cougars are secretive and generally solitary. If two cougars share territory, they will seldom visit the same land at the same time. Since they avoid each other, they rarely fight. Their main prey are deer and elk. However, they will also feed on smaller creatures such as coyotes, porcupines, marmots, beavers, hares, armadillos, birds, and mice. They will even eat berries, grasses, and grasshoppers!

Crane, Japanese *(Grus japonensis)* **T/E**

 Marshlands in portions of China, Siberia, and Korea, and on Hokkaido, the northernmost island of Japan

 The Japanese crane has long, graceful legs. It spends the winter in areas that are very cold, where temperatures drop to minus-four degrees Fahrenheit. In order to stay warm, the bird will stand on one leg; the other leg is tucked into the feathers on its body. Then, after a while, it switches legs. Cranes are well known for their beautiful dance. As they bob their heads, bounce, whirl, and leap, they sometimes pick up objects with their beaks to throw into the air. They like to dance at all times of the year. Often, if one crane in a flock starts to dance, others will follow. Such exuberance seems contagious.

Elephant, Asian *(Elephas maximus)* **E**

 Hilly and mountainous parts of India, Sri Lanka, Indochina, Malaysia, Indonesia, and southern China; also in forested grasslands

 Elephants are viewed with wonder for their huge size, long life, and great intelligence. The elephant's trunk is one of its most fascinating features. With it, the elephant can feed on the ground or overhead. An elephant drinks with its trunk, too, by sucking in the water and squirting it out into its mouth—up to ten quarts of water at a time. Sometimes an elephant gives itself a shower by spraying the water across its back. An elephant can smell things with its trunk. By holding its trunk up to sniff the air, an elephant can catch the scent of predators nearby.

Frigatebird, magnificent *(Fregata magnificens)*

 Seacoasts of the tropical Atlantic, Gulf of Mexico, and eastern Pacific; also found in Africa

 The frigatebird is a large tropical seabird with a wingspan of between eighty-four and ninety-six inches. Its sleek, angled wings allow it to soar high in the sky. In flight, its long, scissor-shaped tail can be seen. The frigatebird is mostly silent. But during breeding season, the males make an unusual noise with their throat pouch, which looks like an inflatable red balloon. By shaking their bills rhythmically against this pouch, they produce a drumming sound.

Giraffe *(Giraffa camelopardalis)*

 Open woodlands and dry savannas in Africa south of the Sahara

 The giraffe is known for its long neck. At a standing height of about nineteen feet, it is the world's tallest land mammal. Drinking water from the ground with such a long neck is tricky for giraffes. To make matters worse, their hind legs are much shorter than their front ones. They must stretch their forelegs way out or kneel down in order to reach for a drink. The coat of each individual giraffe has its own particular markings. Like a fingerprint in humans, this pattern distinguishes a giraffe from all others of its species.

Gorilla *(Gorilla gorilla)* T/E

 Rain forests of western Africa

 Gorillas are the largest of all primates. Mature male gorillas are called silverbacks. Some of them may grow to be nearly six feet tall and weigh about four hundred pounds. They are very strong. They show their strength by beating their chests and charging at any animal that threatens them. Such actions have given gorillas an undeserved reputation for being ferocious, but they are actually no more aggressive than any other wild animal. In fact, they are usually quite gentle. They spend much of the day feeding on a vegetarian diet of leaves and fruit.

Hare, arctic *(Lepus arcticus)*

 Tundra and rocky slopes in northern Canada and Greenland

 Arctic hares, like all hares, are adapted for speed. Their long hind legs and feet make it possible for them to run rapidly. They also flee in a zigzag manner, which helps them to elude predators. When excited, they can leap twelve feet and run more than thirty miles per hour. During the breeding season in the first two weeks of April, male hares box with other males and also with the female hares they are pursuing.

Hippopotamus *(Hippopotamus amphibius)*

 Lake and river habitats in Africa south of the Sahara

 Hippos spend most of the day partially submerged or standing in shallow water. They can remain completely underwater for up to thirty minutes. They like flat, sandy banks for sunbathing. However, hippos must take care not to sun themselves too long. Their sensitive skin can crack and sunburn if it does not remain moist. Yawning hippos can open their mouths very wide. In males, this behavior can be a threatening gesture toward other males.

Impala *(Aepyceros melampus)* E

 Open woodland, savanna, and sandy bush country in western Africa

 Impalas are graceful animals of the antelope family. The males have distinctive and beautiful lyre-shaped horns. When impalas sense danger, they run away almost effortlessly. They easily leap over bushes and over one another, too, as they go. Sometimes they spring high into the air, even if there is no obstacle in their path. They can also jump fairly substantial distances. People have seen impalas, racing across the savanna, that bounded first twenty-six feet, then sixteen feet, and finally thirty feet in succession!

Jaguar *(Panthera onca)* T

 Rain forests and grasslands in Central and South America

 The jaguar is at home in both the jungle and the savanna. But jaguars like to bathe and swim, so they never stray far away from water. They are fine swimmers and can easily cross wide streams. Jaguars hunt many animals that are also found in or near water, such as the capybara and the tapir. They even are said to have attacked crocodiles and caimans. Jaguars can climb trees well but generally do their stalking from ground level. Another interesting feature: the jaguar is the only big cat not known to roar; instead, adult jaguars grunt.

Kangaroo, red *(Macropus rufus)*

 Inland plains of Australia

Kangaroos are well known for their great ability to hop. When a kangaroo travels at a slow

pace, it usually jumps about four to six feet at a time. However, when frightened, it can leap more than thirty feet. Adult male red kangaroos engage in ritualized combat to test their strength and skills. They wrestle, hug, box, and kick each other throughout several "rounds" of their fight. These "matches" become more serious during mating season. When a kangaroo kicks its opponent with its hind legs, it keeps its tail on the ground for support.

Leopard *(Panthera pardus)* T/E

 Varies from desert to forest in Africa south of the Sahara and in southern Asia, with small scattered populations in North Africa, the Middle East, and Asia

 Unlike the jaguar, the leopard almost always shares its home territory with a stronger animal such as a lion or tiger. However, leopards are usually solitary creatures. Among all the species of big cats, the leopard is the best climber. Often leopards will rest or nap in the branches of a tree. In Africa, the leopard is considered threatened; everywhere else, it is endangered.

Macaw, green-winged *(Ara chloroptera)*
Macaw, scarlet *(Ara macao)*

 Tropical rain forests of eastern Panama, most of northern South America, and Bolivia, Brazil, and Paraguay

 Macaws fly with relatively slow wingbeats. They often travel in flocks through the rain forest, where they have been seen collecting clay. They eat this substance possibly as a mineral supplement or to detoxify any poisons found in seeds in their diet. They also consume nuts and fruits. Once a male and female macaw pair off, they stay together for life.

Mallard *(Anas platyrhynchos)*

 Bodies of water from bays to marshes in the wild as well as ponds and ditches in urban areas found in North America, Europe, Asia, and Australia

 The mallard is often one of the first wild water birds a human child will see, since mallards frequently intermingle and breed with domestic ducks in city parks. In fact, the mallard is the ancestor of these tame ducks. Males of this species have beautiful iridescent green head feathers for most of the year.

Orangutan *(Pongo pygmaeus)* E

 *Rain forests of Borneo and northern Sumatra*

The orangutan is the only great ape of Asia. Unlike the other great apes, orangutans prefer solitude. They spend most of the day in rain-forest trees. Each night, they build a nest in which to sleep. Orangutans have long, powerful arms and can grasp with both their hands and feet. This allows them to maneuver through the forest easily and to pick fruit, their favored food.

Panda, giant *(Ailuropoda melanoleuca)* E

 Mountainous forests of central China

 The black-and-white fur and cuddly appearance of the panda make it one of the most well-known and well-loved animals in the world. It spends most of its time foraging for bamboo, the only food it eats. Each day, it consumes from twenty to forty-five pounds of leaves and stalks. The panda's front paws are specially adapted for holding this plant. Pandas in the wild prefer to be alone and shuffle about in their shy and gentle way. If they do meet another animal, sometimes they cover their black eye patches with their paws to hide their faces.

Penguin, Adélie *(Pygoscelis adeliae)*

 Coast of Antarctica and many of the Antarctic islands

Adélies stand upright to walk and run on land and ice. However, sometimes they slide across the snow like little toboggans. In the sea, they swim beneath the surface, using their small wings like flippers to reach speeds of fifteen miles per hour. They often "porpoise," or pop out of the water, to heights of around six feet when coming ashore.

Penguin, macaroni *(Eudyptes chrysolophus)*

 Outer and inner islands around Antarctica

The "Macaroni dandies" were eighteenth-century travelers from England who dressed in flamboyant clothing. Years ago, the penguins acquired the name *macaroni* because of the bright yellow crests over their eyes. Macaroni penguins live in colonies and prefer steep terrain. They have rookeries on coastal hills and cliffs. Like all penguins, macaronis cannot fly.

Tiger *(Panthera tigris)* **E**

 Varies from rain forests, mountain forests, mangrove swamps, grasslands, and savannas to rocky and arid areas in Asia

A tiger's stripes are one of its most striking features. However, the stripes also provide excellent camouflage. When standing in front of a background of vegetation such as dried grass, the tiger will "disappear" through optical illusion. Tigers are usually active at night. Although good stalkers and hunters, 90 percent of the time they fail to catch their prey.

Toad, true *(Bufo typhonius)*

 Rain forests in South America

The head of the true toad is uneven, giving it a leaf-like appearance. This camouflage allows it to remain well hidden in a tropical forest. The toad also has other defense mechanisms, including the ability to produce noxious secretions on its skin to ward off would-be attackers.

Whale, humpback *(Megaptera novaeangliae)* **E**

 Oceans and seas of both Northern and Southern Hemispheres

These mammoth creatures are playful and curious. They often breach, or jump out of the water, as they frolic. At times they wave their flippers and slap their tails. They even sing. The tail of the humpback is very special. Each individual whale tail has a unique pattern of black-and-white pigment on its flukes. This pattern is slightly different in every humpback, much as a fingerprint is unique to each human being.

Wolf, gray *(Canis lupus)* **E**

 Both open and forested areas throughout the Northern Hemisphere

Biologists who study wolves have found them to be intelligent, social animals that mate for life. Family members and relatives usually form packs of four to seven wolves, with an alpha male and female as the group's leaders. All animals in the pack help to raise and care for the pups. Wolves howl to gather the pack together, to warn one another of danger, to find one another in unfamiliar territory, to contact one another across great distances, and to establish boundaries with neighboring packs.